C000116631

BOYS
ANTI-TANK
RIFLE

MARK I

2010

The Naval & Military Press Ltd

Published by the
The Naval & Military Press
in association with the Royal Armouries

Unit 10 Ridgewood Industrial Park,
Uckfield, East Sussex, TN22 5QE
Tel: +44 (0) 1825 749494
Fax: +44 (0) 1825 765701

MILITARY HISTORY AT YOUR FINGERTIPS
www.naval-military-press.com

ONLINE GENEALOGY RESEARCH
www.military-genealogy.com

ONLINE MILITARY CARTOGRAPHY
www.militarymaproom.com

The Library & Archives Department at the Royal Armouries Museum, Leeds, specialises in the history and development of armour and weapons from earliest times to the present day. Material relating to the development of artillery and modern fortifications is held at the Royal Armouries Museum, Fort Nelson.

ROYAL
ARMOURIES

For further information contact:
Royal Armouries Museum, Library, Armouries Drive,
Leeds, West Yorkshire LS10 1LT
Royal Armouries, Library, Fort Nelson, Down End Road, Fareham PO17 6AN

Or visit the Museum's website at
www.armouries.org.uk

*In reprinting in facsimile from the original, any imperfections are inevitably reproduced
and the quality may fall short of modern type and cartographic standards.*

CONTENTS

ILLUSTRATIONS

COLOURED CHART SHOWING MECHANISMS, ETC.—
in Pocket on Back Cover

THE BOYS ANTI-TANK RIFLE

BOYS ANTI-TANK RIFLE (MARK I)

DATA

ANTI-TANK RIFLE

Overall length	5 ft. 3¾ in.
Weight (without magazine) . . .	36 lb.
Weight with magazine (unloaded) .	37 lb.
Weight with magazine (loaded) . .	38½ lb.
Length of barrel and body . . .	4 ft. 4 in.
Length of bolt	10¼ in.
Length of extractor	7⅛ in.
Length of ejector	7½ in.
Height of front support	12 in.
Height of foresight (normal) . .	9/10 in.
Height of backsight	13/20 in.
Muzzle velocity	2,640 feet per second.
Maximum height	14 in.
Maximum width	6 in.
Sight radius	2 ft. 10¼ in.
Rifling	7 grooves, right hand.
	1 turn in 10 in.
Extreme range	7,000 yards.

SIGHTS

Foresight.—The foresight is of the blade pattern and there are seven sizes:

−.045-inch ⎫
−.03-inch ⎬ These foresights are lower than the normal
−.015-inch ⎭ foresight by the amount shown.

Normal.

.015-inch ⎫
.03-inch ⎬ These foresights are higher than the normal
.045-inch ⎭ foresight by the amount shown.

Note.—It is important that rifles are zeroed and the proper foresight fixed.

Backsight.—There are two types in use, one being a fixed aperture for use up to 300 yards, and the other a movable backsight. Method of adjusting is as follows:

For ranges up to 300 yards: move lever to the left.

For ranges from 300 to 500 yards: move lever to the right.

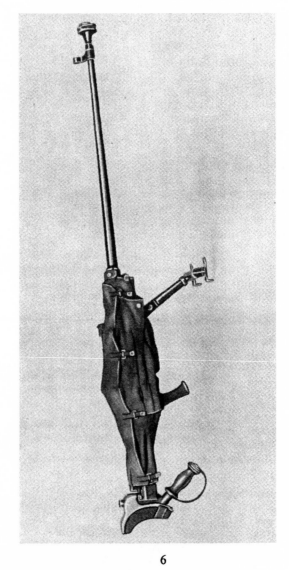

THE BOYS ANTI-TANK RIFLE WITH BREECH COVER IN POSITION

MAGAZINE

Overhead box type, capacity . . . . 5 rounds.
Overhead box type, weight (empty) . . . 1 lb.
Overhead box type, weight (filled) . . . 2½ lb.

AMMUNITION

.55-inch.
In shape is similar to the rimless .300 ammunition, but is very
much larger.
Weight: 5 oz.
Length (complete round): 5¼ in.

GENERAL DESCRIPTION

After the Battle of France the returning members of the B.E.F.
had many hard things to say about this weapon, the general
impression being that as a weapon designed to stop modern
tanks it was out of date, but—and this is a fact that cannot be
avoided—it was never intended to stop modern tanks.

This weapon was designed to afford a means of protection
against light armoured fighting vehicles, *i.e.*, the type of vehicle
which the Home Guard are likely to have to deal with, certainly
in the early stages of either an air-borne or sea-borne landing on
our coasts.

It is very important that the Home Guard realize this before
doubts arise as to its capabilities. An example to prove this point
is that one would never think of putting into a boxing ring a
bantam-weight to fight a heavy-weight unless one desired the
complete annihilation of the bantam-weight.

In our study of this weapon it is vital to get to know what it
can do, how and when it can do it, and, having grasped that, not
to expect miracles from it. Realizing the job it is designed for, it
is a first-class weapon—in fact, there isn't a better.

CHARACTERISTICS

To know what a weapon will do one must have a knowledge
of its main characteristics. These are :
  (i) Extremely accurate at ranges of 300 yards and below.
  (ii) Good penetration (see " Penetrations ").
  (iii) Emits an obvious muzzle flash, which must be con-
      sidered when siting this weapon.

(iv) Creates a distinct muzzle blast, which is also a factor to be borne in mind when siting.

(v) It is reasonably light, enabling it to be moved quickly from one position to another.

PENETRATIONS

When to fire? This can be decided only by the firer, having a clear knowledge of the penetrative powers of the .55 bullet.

Range	Bullet making a direct hit		Bullet striking at an angle of 20 degrees		Bullet striking at an angle of 40 degrees	
Yards	Inches	M/M.	Inches	M/M.	Inches	M/M.
100	.91	23.2	.67	17.0	.43	11.0
300	.82	20.9	.63	16.0	.38	9.6
500	.74	18.8	.60	15.3	.35	8.8

This weapon is also useful for penetrating houses and sand-bag emplacements. The maximum penetration to be expected in this form of firing is:

    (i) Brick walls . . . . 14 inches.
    (ii) Sandbags . . . . 10 inches.

NOTE.—**It is important to realize that the range to the target is not the only factor in answering the question " When to fire? " The second, and perhaps the more important, is " When can I be** CERTAIN **of getting penetration? " This is governed by the firer's determination not to fire until he is sure of a kill.**

MAGAZINE

The magazine platform of this rifle has a raised portion which prevents the bolt being closed when the magazine is empty.

The effect of this is to prevent the man having practice in bolt manipulation unless dummy rounds are available.

Where dummy rounds are not available the bolt can be made to operate by the insertion of a half-penny under the lips of the magazine, thus enabling the man to obtain the practice necessary for quick reloading without which fire effect must necessarily be reduced.

Home Guard personnel will have little chance of firing this weapon at the proper ranges owing to the great distances the .55 bullet travels. It is interesting to note that it reaches twice as far as the .300 bullet. There are, naturally, few ranges which have the required danger area. This does not, however, prevent practice being obtained, and there are two recognized methods:

    (i) 1/30th scale, firing with .22 ammunition.

   (ii) Firing at 25 yards into an open range stop butt.

        Note.—The ordinary 30-yards range is unsuitable until strengthened to prevent penetration.

MAIN PARTS

(*a*) Recoil reducer (1).

(*b*) Barrel (2).

(*c*) Foresight bracket and foresight (3).

(*d*) Body (4).

(*e*) Cradle (5).

(*f*) Trunnion (6).

(*g*) Front support (7).

(*h*) Pistol grip (8).

(*i*) Backsight bracket and backsight (9).

(*j*) Cheek rest (10).

(*k*) Shoulder piece (11).

(*l*) Shoulder piece grip (12).

(*m*) Oil bottle (13).

REMOVING AND REPLACING THE BOLT

REMOVING

The safety catch on this rifle is located at the rear of the body (4) and on the left-hand side.

Push the safety catch forward, raise the bolt lever to its highest position and withdraw the bolt completely to the rear.

The ejector stop is situated just in rear of the magazine catch and immediately over the bolt. Press the ejector stop with the thumb of the left hand and remove the bolt from the body.

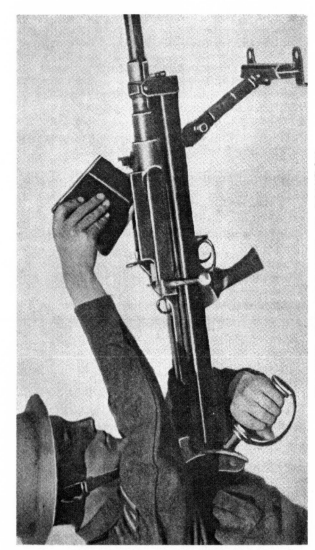

PLACING THE MAGAZINE IN POSITION

REPLACING

Before attempting to replace the bolt, the following points must be noted:

    (i) Hold the bolt with the knob of the bolt lever upwards and pointing to the right.

    (ii) Ensure that the ring of the cocking piece (15) is vertical and in alignment with the lower portion of the bolt lever.

    (iii) The ejector (16) must be on top of the bolt, and in line with the lower portion of the bolt lever. This will automatically position the extractor (17) correctly.

Lay the bolt on the bolt way, taking care that it is perfectly flat. Push the bolt forward as far as it will go, then turn the bolt lever down to the right. It is important to ensure that it is completely pressed down.

The mainspring (20) should now be released by pressing the trigger (22), and the safety catch will be applied by rotating it to the rear.

PLACING ON AND REMOVING THE MAGAZINE

PLACING ON

Hold the magazine in the right hand, fingers on the right-hand side, thumb on the left, with the larger portion of the magazine to the rear and the magazine platform downwards.

Tilt the rear of the magazine upwards, inserting the forward portion into the magazine way, allowing the two lugs on the forward position of the magazine to rest on the sides of the magazine way. Push the magazine fully forward, pressing the rear portion downwards until it is engaged by the magazine catch.

REMOVING

Place the palm of the right hand in rear of the magazine catch, the fingers and thumb assuming a similar position to that when placing on.

Press the magazine catch with the palm, when the rear of the magazine will be released. The magazine can now be removed.

STRIPPING AND ASSEMBLING THE BOLT

It is of the utmost importance that no attempt be made to strip or interfere with the bolt. Misfires will occur if this instruction is not complied with.

The stripping and assembling of the bolt must only be carried out by a qualified armourer.

MECHANISM

OPENING THE BREECH AND WITHDRAWING THE BOLT

On raising the bolt lever, the locking shoulders on the bolt disengage from the recess in the body (4). This action also withdraws the bolt slightly by the action of the bolt lever bearing against the rear surface of the body, permitting primary extraction.

This movement also causes the cocking piece to be forced back by the cam on the bolt, thus withdrawing the striker from the face of the bolt.

On withdrawing the bolt farther to the rear, the ejector stop enters the slot in the ejector (16) and holds it. As the bolt still has a short distance to travel, the ejector pushes the empty case off the face of the bolt. It then falls through the opening in the bottom of the body. The ejector stop prevents further movement of the bolt to the rear.

ON PRESSING THE TRIGGER

On pressure being applied, the trigger (22) rotates and lifts the trigger pawl (23). The head of the trigger pawl bears against the underside of the head of the sear (25), allowing the sear to rotate, thus disengaging it from the cocking piece.

The cocking piece and striker now fly forward under the influence of the compressed mainspring (20).

The trigger pawl is held in the upward position by the trigger spring (24) and the bearing pin in the pistol grip (8).

ON CLOSING THE BREECH

On pushing the bolt forward, the ejector strikes the base of the cartridge in the magazine, forcing it into the chamber. The bolt lever comes up against the face on the rear of the body. The cam projection on the front of the bolt is now in line with the recess in the body (4).

The action of pressing the bolt lever downwards brings the cam surfaces in contact, drawing the bolt forward against the base of the cartridge.

The locking shoulders on the bolt are now in alignment with the locking recesses in the body.

When the bolt lever is fully pressed down the breech is sealed.

During the forward movement the cocking piece was held back by the sear, thus compressing the mainspring and cocking the action.

ON APPLYING THE SAFETY CATCH

On turning the safety catch to the rear it engages in the bolt and on the cocking piece, thus preventing the bolt lever from being raised or the cocking piece withdrawn.

Should the action be cocked when the safety catch is applied, the upper projection will prevent the cocking piece going forward.

RECOIL

The reducing of the effects of the recoil is obtained as follows:

    (i) Recoil reducer (1).

    (ii) Buffer spring (27).

    (iii) Sorbo pad on shoulder piece (11).

A portion of the gases passes along the base and strikes the rear face of the deflector, thus tending to force the barrel forward, so reducing recoil.

On the shock of discharge taking place, the barrel recoils and compresses the buffer spring, thus reducing the recoil transmitted to the firer to a minimum.

Such recoil as is transmitted to the firer is eased considerably by the Sorbo pad on the shoulder piece.

FRONT SUPPORT

The front support (7) has been designed to:

    (i) Give support to the rifle.

    (ii) Permit of the barrel being elevated or depressed.

The following main parts are incorporated in the front support:

    (a) Pivot.

    (b) Hinge.

13

(*c*) Catch.

(*d*) Sleeve.

(*e*) Foot.

Invariably the rifle will be fired with the front support resting on its foot. Occasions, however, may occur when it will be necessary to fold the front support under the rifle. This can be done by pressing the front support catch and at the same time drawing the front support backwards and upwards towards the barrel.

To elevate the barrel, rotate the sleeve in a clockwise direction —to depress the barrel rotate the sleeve in the opposite direction.

MAGAZINE

This is an overhead box type consisting of the following parts:

(*a*) Case.

(*b*) Plate.

(*c*) Platform.

(*d*) Spring.

The occasions on which it will be necessary to strip the magazine for cleaning will be rare, and serious damage will occur if continual stripping is allowed.

STRIPPING THE MAGAZINE

Disengage the stud on the plate. Draw the plate clear of the case, taking care to prevent the spring from flying out. Withdraw the spring and platform.

ASSEMBLING OF MAGAZINE

Position the platform in the case and compress the spring. Slide the plate on to the case, when the stud should reposition itself. Should it fail to do so, a tap with the hand will normally bring it into position.

MAGAZINE FILLING AND EMPTYING

FILLING

The following positions may be adopted for filling:

(*a*) Kneeling on both knees—magazine resting on thigh.

(*b*) Kneeling on one knee—magazine resting on knee.

(*c*) Sitting—magazine resting on thigh or ground.

(*d*) Lying—magazine resting on the ground.

The position to be adopted will depend on circumstances.

Adopt the required position, holding the magazine in the hand with the narrowest portion of the magazine towards the body. Take a cartridge in the other hand, holding it with the base of the cartridge pointing towards the magazine.

Press down on the platform with the thumb of the hand holding the magazine. Place the cartridge on the magazine, base just clear of the magazine lips. Press the cartridge downwards and forwards until positioned under the magazine lips; repeat this action until the magazine is filled with five rounds.

Note.—To fill a magazine correctly and with speed requires much practice. The standard to be aimed at is a complete filling in 20 seconds.

EMPTYING

Hold the magazine with the base of the rounds uppermost. Using another round, place the side of the bullet on the base of the round in the magazine and force it downwards and out of the magazine. Continue this action until the magazine is empty.

LOADING AND UNLOADING

Note.—The actions of loading are explained here with the firer in the lying position. The actions, however, may be performed in any service position.

LOADING

Lie down behind the rifle, body in direct alignment with it, legs close together.

Push the safety catch forward, and place on the magazine. Open and close the breech, remembering the point that the bolt lever must be pressed right down. Apply the safety catch.

The right hand must now be placed on the pistol grip (8), thumb on the left, forefinger along the outside of the trigger guard, remaining fingers round the front and pointing backwards.

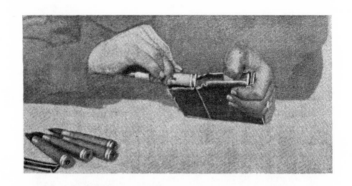

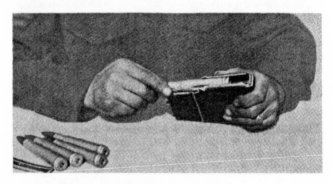

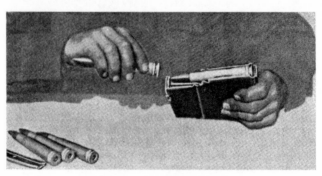

FILLING THE MAGAZINE
16

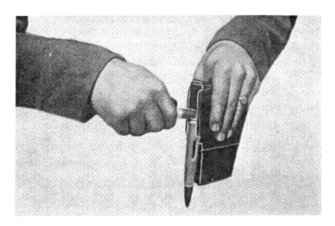

EMPTYING THE MAGAZINE

The left hand grips the shoulder piece grip (12), thumb underneath, fingers on top.

UNLOADING

Push the safety catch forward, remove the magazine, open and close the breech, press the trigger, apply the safety catch and stand clear.

HOLDING, SIGHT SETTING, AIMING AND FIRING

HOLDING

Raise the shoulder piece into the shoulder, making certain it is in firm contact. Lower the cheek on to the cheek rest, place the forefinger of the right hand on the trigger and take the first pressure.

The grip must be a firm one, and it is better to keep the elbows clear of the cover. This will not be possible if firing from the lying position. The advantage to be gained from having the elbows clear is that it enables a better swing to be taken when dealing with moving targets.

SIGHT SETTING

When the rifle has a movable backsight, adjust sights by moving either to the right or the left.

THE CORRECT HOLD

AIMING (STATIONARY TARGET)

The rules to be observed are as follows:

(*a*) Keep the sights upright.

(*b*) Look through the aperture and align the top of the foresight in the centre of the target. Endeavour to keep the
aim in the centre of the aperture.

Note.—The above rules also apply to targets which are
directly approaching or retiring.

AIMING (MOVING TARGET)

The rules to be observed are as follows:

When the target is *moving directly* across the front of the rifle

(*a*) Keep the sights upright.

(*b*) Look through the aperture and align the foresight one
target's width in front of the target and in line with the
centre of it. Endeavour to maintain this aim in the
centre of the aperture.

When the target is *moving obliquely*

(*a*) Keep the sights upright.

(*b*) Look through the aperture and align the foresight on
the front edge of the target and in line with the centre
of it. Endeavour to maintain this aim in the centre of
the aperture.

18

Note.—When aiming at a moving target the swing must be even and must not be checked at the moment of taking the second pressure.

FIRING

The method of firing is the same as with the .300 rifle. The grip must be firmer than that with the ordinary rifle.

Once a round has been fired there must be instant reloading. This is most important, and must be practised until a high standard of efficiency is reached, otherwise a second shot may not be possible.

Having fired the last round in the magazine, and on attempting to reload, it will be found that the bolt will not go forward owing to the bolt coming in contact with the raised portion of the magazine platform.

This raised portion lies in front of the rear portion of the magazine. Unless the bolt is withdrawn fully to the rear it will be found impossible to place on another magazine because the front end of the bolt will prevent the rear portion of the magazine from entering the magazine way.

The point to note here is—on the magazine becoming empty, ensure that the bolt is fully withdrawn to the rear before attempting to place on another magazine.

A CORRECT AIM FOR

A STATIONARY
TANK

A TANK CROSSING

FROM LEFT TO RIGHT   FROM RIGHT TO LEFT

OR

A TANK
APPROACHING
OBLIQUELY

19

SITTING POSITION

KNEELING POSITION

STANDING POSITION

FIRING POSITIONS AND SITING

The positions which give the best results and assist materially in obtaining good fire effect are :

(i) Sitting.

(ii) Kneeling.

(iii) Standing.

The lying position can be used, but is not suitable for getting the best results, particularly against moving targets.

The arc through which the rifle can be swung when in the lying position is so very small that little fire effect can be expected.

When siting the rifle for a particular task, the following points must be borne in mind :

(i) Ability to hit the flank and rear of the target.

(ii) The field of fire should be adequate.

(iii) The utmost use should be made of any available cover.

(iv) Remember the characteristics mentioned previously— muzzle flash and muzzle blast—and allow for them.

(v) An alternative position must be selected and a route to it reconnoitred.

The position selected will normally be occupied by two men, one the firer, the other the observer. The latter should also take on the role of protector for the former. It must be borne in mind that the rifle can be fired successfully without the observer being present.

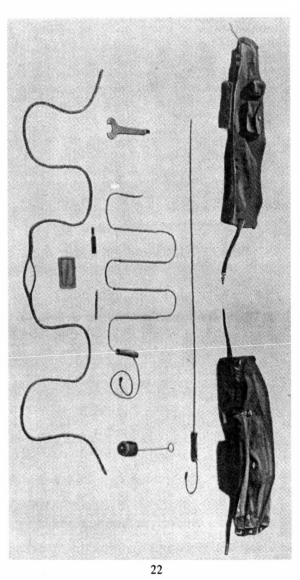

THE CLEANING OUTFIT

CLEANING

Breech Cover.—The cover affords protection for the body and mechanism and should be kept on the rifle whenever it is not actually in use. It also acts as a hold-all for the cleaning materials.

Cleaning Rod.—The rod is sectioned to permit of its being carried in the breech cover.

It consists of handle, through which is the cord, attached to the handle is one of the sections of the rod. There are three other sections, the cord passing through each. At the end of the rod there is a small section which is externally threaded to take the loop.

To assemble, hold the handle in the left hand and pull the cord. This has the effect of joining up all the sectioned pieces. To enable it to be retained in position, fix the cord in the slot provided in the handle.

The rod is carried in the long pocket on the right-hand side of the breech cover.

Loop.—This is a solid brass tube internally threaded at one end for securing to the rod. The other end has an eyelet for the insertion of the flannelette.

The loop is carried in the pocket on the left-hand side of the breech cover; flannelette may also be carried in this pocket.

Pullthrough.—This consists of a 9-foot length of rope with a loop in the centre to take either gauze or flannelette.

If no rod is available it would be carried in the long pocket on the right-hand side of the breech cover.

Gauze.—This is a piece of fine wire mesh $3\frac{1}{2}$ in. by $3\frac{1}{4}$ in. It will be used in exactly the same way as the gauze is used on the Service rifle.

The gauze is carried in the same pocket as the loop.

Wire Brush.—This is a very stiff wire brush, used for cleaning the barrel. At one end there is a small brass tube internally threaded to enable it to be connected to the cleaning rod.

This brush is carried in the same pocket as the loop.

Bristle Brush.—The brush is secured to a long wire handle. It is used for cleaning the chamber.

This brush is carried with the cleaning rod.

Combination Tool.—This tool is shaped like a spanner at one end, to be used for the removal of the recoil reducer (this should only be removed by a qualified armourer). The other end is bent and shaped like a screwdriver to permit the removal of the deflector.

The combination tool is carried with the cleaning rod.

TO CLEAN THE RIFLE

Remove the bolt and magazine, remove the deflector from the recoil reducer by unscrewing the screws, using the combination tool.

All dirt, old oil and fouling should be removed from both the deflector and the recoil reducer. Once cleaned it should be left in a slightly oiled condition.

Clean the barrel in a similar way to cleaning a Service rifle, using the cleaning rod; the size of the flannelette to be 6 in. by 4 in. Re-oil the barrel, using oily flannelette 4 in. by 4 in.

The chamber will be cleaned with the bristle brush, which should be surrounded by flannelette to prevent the brush getting too dirty to clean the chamber.

All other parts of the rifle will be dry-cleaned and then left in a slightly oily condition.

As with the Service rifle, the barrel and chamber should be dry before firing. It is also advisable to dry out the recoil reducer, but it is realized that this will not always be possible.

ATTACHMENT FOR BOYS ANTI-TANK RIFLE TO PERMIT FIRING WITH .22 AMMUNITION

GENERAL

To enable men to get sufficient practice in aiming and swinging with the Boys anti-tank rifle an attachment has been designed which, when fitted to the Boys anti-tank rifle and a .22 rifle, allows this practice and at the same time fires .22 ammunition.

This attachment consists of the following:

(a) Front bracket (30).

(b) Rear bracket (31).

(c) Plate (32).

(d) Clamp with wing nuts (33).

(e) Trigger connector (34).

DESCRIPTION

FRONT BRACKET

The front bracket is a clamping attachment for fitting to the barrel of the anti-tank rifle; it also acts as a support for the nose-cap of the .22 rifle.

It consists of a semi-circular portion, which is slotted to fit over the foresight bracket. This semi-circular portion has a right-hand extension, which is also slotted to take the bayonet standard of the .22 rifle.

REAR BRACKET

The rear bracket is attached to the butt of the .22 rifle and to the anti-tank rifle.

It is a flat, iron bar, to which is riveted a semi-circular fitting lined with leather. This part is set at an angle to take the small of the butt of the .22 rifle. An elongated slot is situated in the centre of the iron bar.

PLATE

The object of this is to attach the rear bracket to the anti-tank rifle.

The plate is a flat, iron bar; it has a hole in the centre, and each end is recessed to permit fitting to the upper tubes of the anti-tank rifle.

25

ATTACHMENT FOR BOYS A/TK. RIFLE
TO PERMIT FIRING WITH .22 RIFLE AMMUNITION

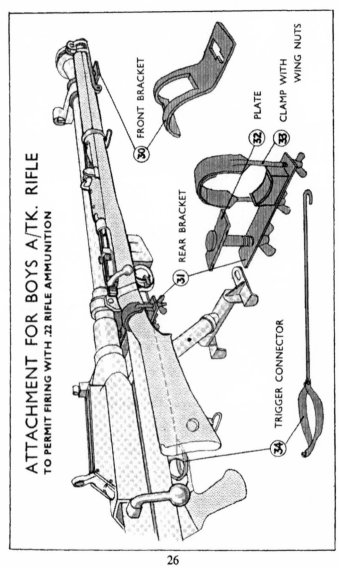

30 FRONT BRACKET

31 REAR BRACKET

32 PLATE

33 CLAMP WITH WING NUTS

34 TRIGGER CONNECTOR

26

CLAMP

This portion clamps the butt of the .22 rifle to the semi-circular portion of the rear bracket.

The clamp is U-shaped, lined with leather, and at each it is screwed to take the wing nuts.

TRIGGER CONNECTOR

The purpose of this is to connect the trigger of the anti-tank rifle with the trigger of the .22 rifle.

The portion known as the clip fits behind the trigger of the anti-tank rifle. The two arms of the clip pass on each side of the anti-tank rifle trigger guard.

Attached to the clip by nut and bolt is a thin rod. This rod passes from the clip to the trigger of the .22 rifle, the end of the rod being shaped to fit round the trigger of the .22 rifle.

ASSEMBLY

Hold the front bracket with the extending portion pointing to the right and attach it to the anti-tank rifle.

Insert the plate between the barrel and the frame tubes immediately in rear of the trunnion.

Hold the rear bracket under the frame tubes and immediately below the plate. Insert the screw in the elongated slot and into the threaded hole in the plate and screw up.

Place the bayonet standard of the .22 rifle in the slotted portion of the front bracket; draw the .22 rifle back about half an inch.

Lower the butt of the .22 rifle on to the rear bracket. Place the clamp over the small of the butt and screw up to the rear bracket.

Attach the clip in rear of the trigger of the anti-tank rifle; attach the rod to the clip by means of the nut and bolt. Pass the rod to the trigger of the .22 rifle and hook it on.

ADJUSTMENT

Adjust the length of the trigger connector to allow the cocking piece of the .22 rifle to be released when the trigger of the anti-tank rifle is pressed, and secure the clamp.

Lateral adjustment of the .22 rifle is obtained by slightly unscrewing the thumb screw of the rear bracket and moving the butt in the required direction. When correctly positioned screw up the thumb screw.

Adjustment for elevation will not be necessary, as the front bracket is so fitted that the correct elevation is automatically obtained.

ZEROING

Load the .22 rifle. Aim and fire the anti-tank rifle. The shot should hit the selected mark. If it does not, adjust the .22 rifle as previously explained and fire again until the aim of the anti-tank rifle and the shot of the .22 rifle coincide.

THE STANDARD MINIATURE 1/30 SCALE RANGE

The following points must be borne in mind when constructing the apparatus necessary for a range of this type:

    (i) On a scale of 1/30th, a representative tank target 4.4 in. by 2 in., moving at 1 foot per second at a range of 15 yards, would represent a light tank, size about $11\frac{1}{2}$ feet, travelling across the line of the anti-tank rifle at 20 miles per hour at a range of 450 yards.

    (ii) If the representative target has a run of 11 feet, the time taken to complete the run should be 11 seconds. During this time the anti-tank rifle would, at a range of 15 yards, move through an arc of 14 degrees.

    (iii) To be able to judge whether the firer is aiming the required amount in front, scoring areas similar to the representative target must be inscribed in front of the actual target. The distance these scoring areas should be in front and in rear (this enables a run in the opposite direction) of the actual target is the length of the target less .6 of an inch. This correctly allows for the time of flight of the .22 bullet during its 15 yards of flight.

The strawboard on which the target and scoring areas are attached should be 18 in. by 10 in; the target and scoring areas will be 12 in. long.

DESCRIPTION OF APPARATUS

This consists of two uprights about 4 feet high, but if used from the ricochet pit of a 30-yards range would be higher. The uprights are slotted at the top to allow for the laying in of a board 12 feet long.

HOW TO MAKE IT

CROSS BAR

END SUPPORTS

ONE ON FIRING POINT

SMALL SCREW EYES

CORD

NARROW STRIPS OF PLY—WOOD

STRONG CLIPS TO HOLD THE TARGET

APPROX 14"

18"

PAPER TARGET MOUNTED ON CARDBOARD

BRASS HOOK

CORD

12' 6"

CORD

THE STANDARD MINIATURE. 1/30TH SCALE RANGE

The edges of the board form a groove in which a runner travels. The latter is made of hardwood and shaped to travel smoothly in the groove.

On the sides of the runner are screwed two pairs of three-ply brackets, each taking a tin clip, which holds the strawboard on which the target is mounted.

Two cards are attached to hooks on each side of the runner. These pass round hooks at the end of the runner way and are taken back to the firing-point to two winding drums.

One edge of the board forming the running track is straight to allow level movement of the target.

The other edge is shaped. Thus by reversing the board an undulating run will be obtained.

Note.—Any miniature range or 30-yards range is suitable for the erection of this apparatus. The normal safety precautions will be observed.

THE IMPROVISED RANGE

When it is not possible to obtain the apparatus mentioned above, the following improvised apparatus will be found useful:

DESCRIPTION OF APPARATUS

Two lengths of wood (branches of trees will do), about 4½ feet in height and about from 2 to 4 inches thick.

Two spring paper clips (3 inches wide is ideal).

About 40 yards of string (fairly strong).

Three staples.

25 yards of wire (small gauge).

Two 3-inch nails.

ASSEMBLY

Drive the two lengths of wood in the ground about 10 yards apart. Fasten the wire as shown.

Place the staples at the three places marked. These act as guides for the string.

Bend the two 3-inch nails and pass them through the holes in the paper clips. In this position they will hold the strawboard to the wires.

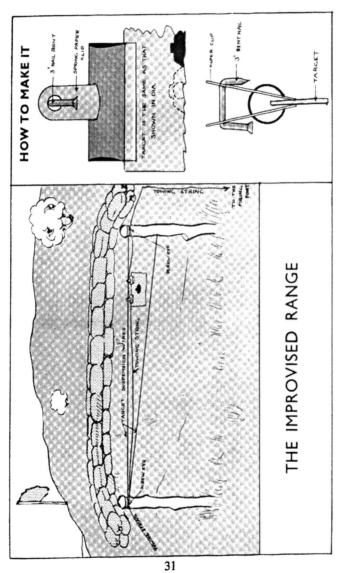

HOW TO MAKE IT

3" NAIL BENT

SPRING PAPER CLIP

TARGET IS THE SAME AS THAT SHOWN IN DIA.

PAPER CLIP

3" BENT NAIL

TARGET

TOWING STRING

TO THE FIRING POINT

SCREW EYE

TARGET SUSPENSION WIRES

TOWING STRING

SCREW EYE

THE IMPROVISED RANGE

BOYS ANTI-TANK RIFLE MK. I.

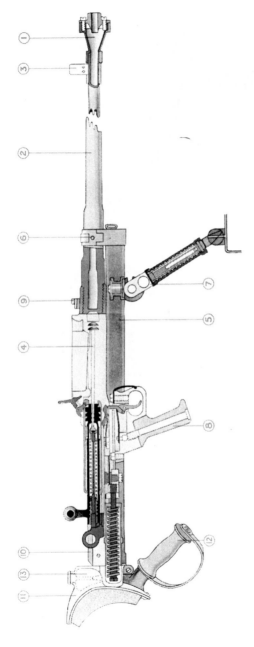

1. RECOIL REDUCER.
2. BARREL.
3. FORESIGHT BRACKET AND FORESIGHT.
4. BODY.
5. CRADLE.
6. TRUNNION.
7. FRONT SUPPORT.
8. PISTOL GRIP.
9. BACKSIGHT BRACKET AND BACKSIGHT.
10. CHEEK REST.
11. SHOULDER PIECE.
12. SHOULDER PIECE GRIP.
13. OIL BOTTLE.

BOLT

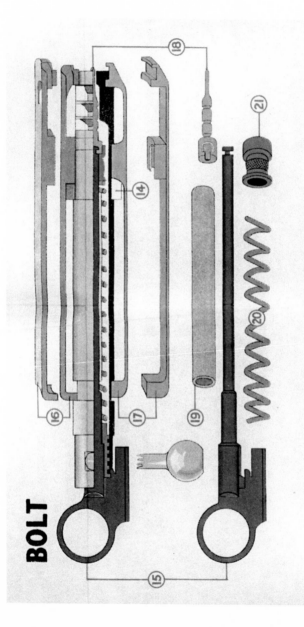

⑭ BOLT RING.
⑮ COCKING PIECE.
⑯ EJECTOR.
⑰ EXTRACTOR.
⑱ STRIKER.
⑲ STRIKER SPRING SLEEVE.
⑳ MAINSPRING.
㉑ STRIKER SLEEVE.

PISTOL GRIP AND TRIGGER MECHANISM

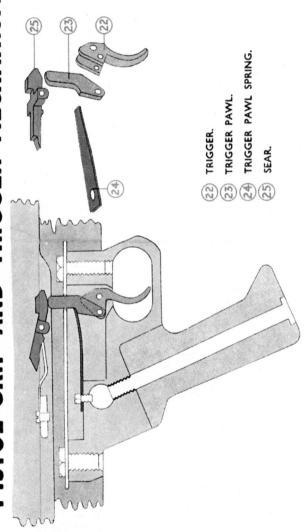

- ㉒ TRIGGER.
- ㉓ TRIGGER PAWL.
- ㉔ TRIGGER PAWL SPRING.
- ㉕ SEAR.

BUFFER

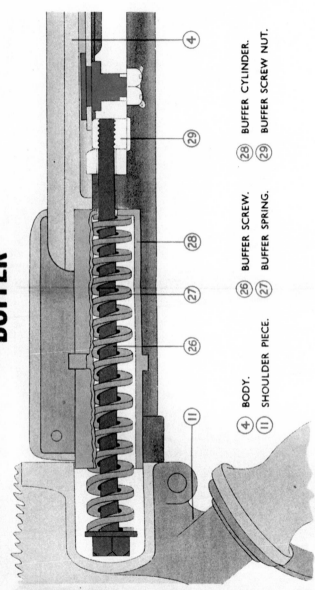

4 BODY.
11 SHOULDER PIECE.
26 BUFFER SCREW.
27 BUFFER SPRING.
28 BUFFER CYLINDER.
29 BUFFER SCREW NUT.

Lightning Source UK Ltd.
Milton Keynes UK
01 April 2010

152212UK00001B/24/P